to Cindi Tran
I wish you and your
family the best life
has to offer...

Treasures Within

Zia Oboodiyat & Jim Lemon

Contacting the authors

ZIA OBOODIYAT
40087 MISSION BLVD. SUITE 204
FREMONT, CA 94539-3680

ZINSTEINE@AOL.COM

JAMES J LEMON, JAMES J LEMON GRAPHICS
141 S CALIFORNIA AVE, NO. B306
PALO ALTO, CA 94306

LEMONJIM@JJLG.COM

COPYRIGHT ©2005
ZIA OBOODIYAT & JAMES J LEMON

ALL RIGHTS RESERVED. NO PART OF THIS WORK MAY BE REPRODUCED OR USED IN ANY FORMS OR BY ANY MEANS - GRAPHIC, ELECTRONIC OR MECHANICAL, INCLUDING PHOTOCOPYING OR INFORMATION STORAGE AND RETRIEVAL SYSTEMS - WITHOUT WRITTEN PERMISSION FROM THE COPYRIGHT HOLDERS.

PUBLISHED BY ZIA OBOODIAT & JAMES J LEMON GRAPHICS

VISIT HTTP://WWW.JJLG.COM

ISBN 10: 1-59975-574-2
ISBN 13: 978-1-59975-574-8

PRINTED IN THE UNITED STATES BY FALCON BOOKS, SAN RAMON, CA

Treasures Within

POETRY BY ZIA OBOODIYAT

IMAGES BY JIM LEMON

Zia Oboodiyat — Preface

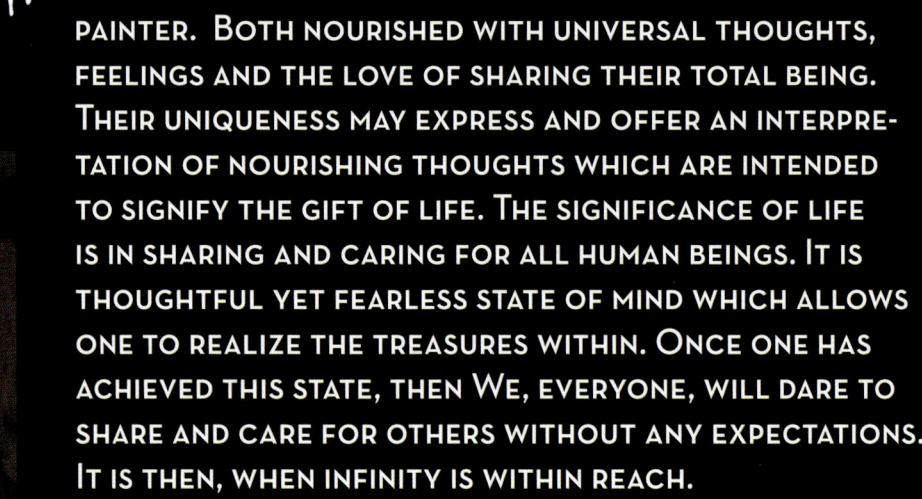

Cries in the eyes of a poet, the brush strokes of a painter. Both nourished with universal thoughts, feelings and the love of sharing their total being. Their uniqueness may express and offer an interpretation of nourishing thoughts which are intended to signify the gift of life. The significance of life is in sharing and caring for all human beings. It is thoughtful yet fearless state of mind which allows one to realize the treasures within. Once one has achieved this state, then We, everyone, will dare to share and care for others without any expectations. It is then, when infinity is within reach.

I wish to dedicate this book to my daughter Natalie and my son Nathan, for they have fed my soul with their unconditional love and affection. Special thanks to Tom and Shideh McDonald, Chip and Laura Koehler and my family who have been generous with their help and love. I also acknowledge my long time friend Jim Lemon whose innovative graphic arts awaken one's mind and heart. Finally to all of you who have been a guiding light in my life, who have touched my soul and who have shared with and cared for the human race. I wish for all of you Love, Unity, Peace and Justice

Jim Lemon

It's a priveledge to work with Zia, making this compilation of images and words. Hurried meetings and fleeting glimmers and daunting difficulties may have loomed, but we are prevailing! Sometimes there is a perfect match and sometimes the contrast, or lack of it, that can convey a message. In the final analysis, the measure of joy is always worth the effort. All my work is pro-bono and completely free to Zia and his beloved charity.

So, Let's get on with the show!

Contents

2	Preface
3	Contents
4	Behold
6	I Favor My Right Hand
9	Listen to the Silence
10	Peace
12	The Solid Rock
14	The Beauty of Life
17	Cruel Cycle
19	You are Now in My Heart
21	Fantasy
23	Hope
24	Internal Treasures
26	Limits of Life
28	Exposure
30	Only You
31	We Are All One
32	Friendship Through My Eyes
33	Experience
34	The Structure of Love
36	It Matters Not
37	My Mind
38	The Road towards Unity
39	Fear
40	The Flight towards oneness
42	Ambitious but Lonely
	I Am Happy
44	Love Comse Through Within
47	Love is to be Shared
49	Fruitless Tree
50	Drifters Drift
52	Be Fair
54	The Turbulent Mind
56	The Secret of Life
58	I Kissed You
59	The Wise Thorn
60	Tears
62	The Windows
63	The Cat
64	A Hollow in Space
66	The Joy of Flight
68	The Origin
70	A Larger Life
72	Reflection
74	The Universe Within Me
76	Birth of a Thought
78	The Old Man
80	A Shattered Mind
82	Cemeteries
84	The Heart of My Soul
86	The Rainbow
87	In the Garden of Life
	Friendly Advice
88	Where all the Angels Fly
90	Meaning of Life
91	Treasures Within
92	The Structure of Love
94	I Know I Love You
96	Father I Am Proud
98	Hello Ocean
	I Have Given Myself to the Ocean
100	The Parellel Universe
101	Colophon

Behold

Listen to the voice of the sea
For it speaks the language of the ages
Listen to its roaring waves
That they spread out the unspoken stories
and listen to their request

Which is to behold all glories.

I Favor My Right Hand

I am a right-handed man
not because

my right hand is white or my left hand is black, but
because I am a right handed man.
I favor my right hand
not because

my right hand is American or my left hand is from
Iran, but because I am a right handed man.
I favor my right hand
not because

the left hand is shorter or the right hand is longer
nor because

Image: anHandforest.004

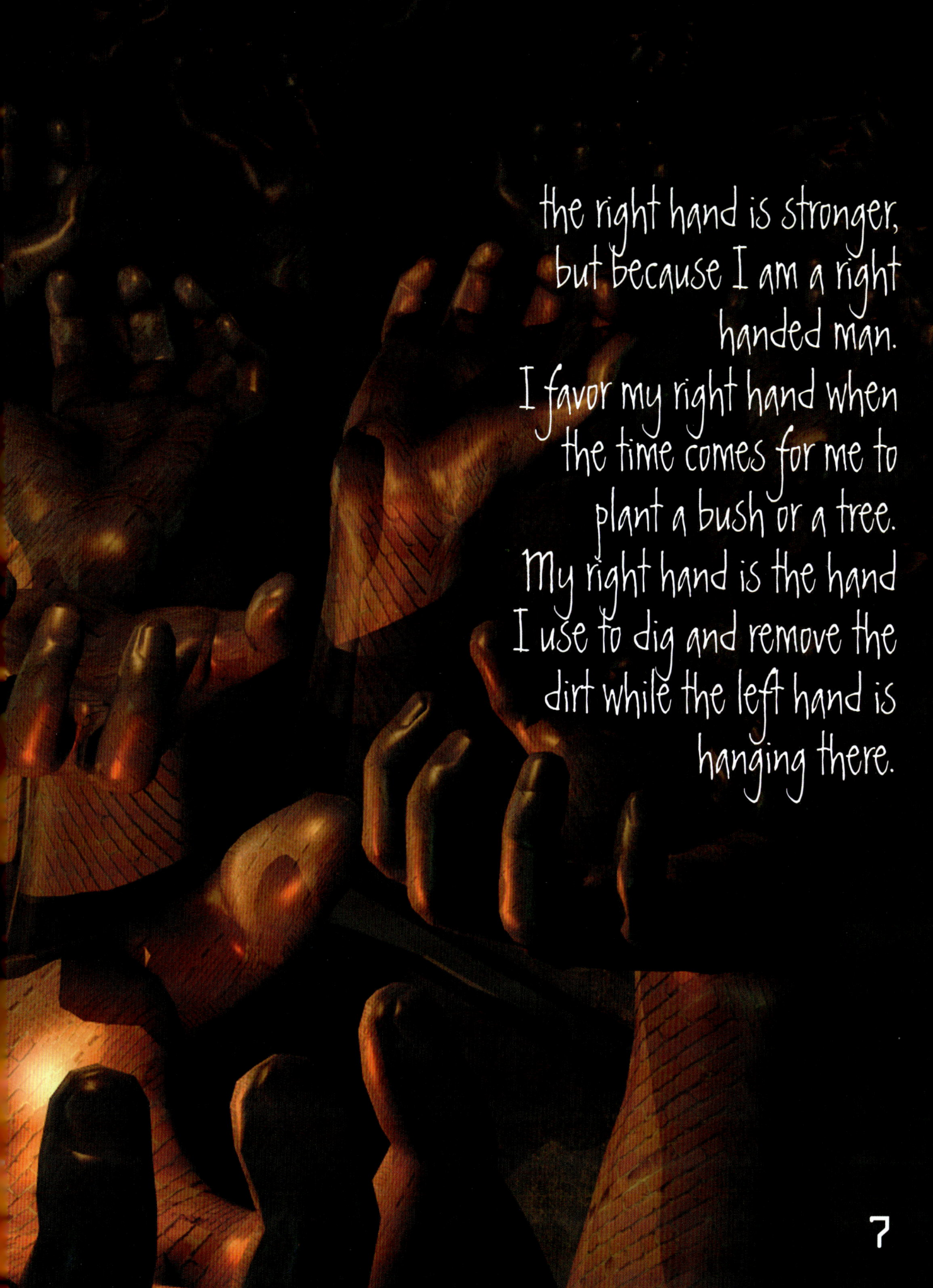

the right hand is stronger, but because I am a right handed man. I favor my right hand when the time comes for me to plant a bush or a tree. My right hand is the hand I use to dig and remove the dirt while the left hand is hanging there.

Image: D2179C

Listen to the Silence

Listen to the heart beats
of an unborn child
feel the growth of a rose
and its beauty
when you see the seed
listen to the silence
that serenity holds within
listen to the whisper of wind
that caries with it
the history of ages
wrap yourself with love
and feel the warmth
of awareness within.

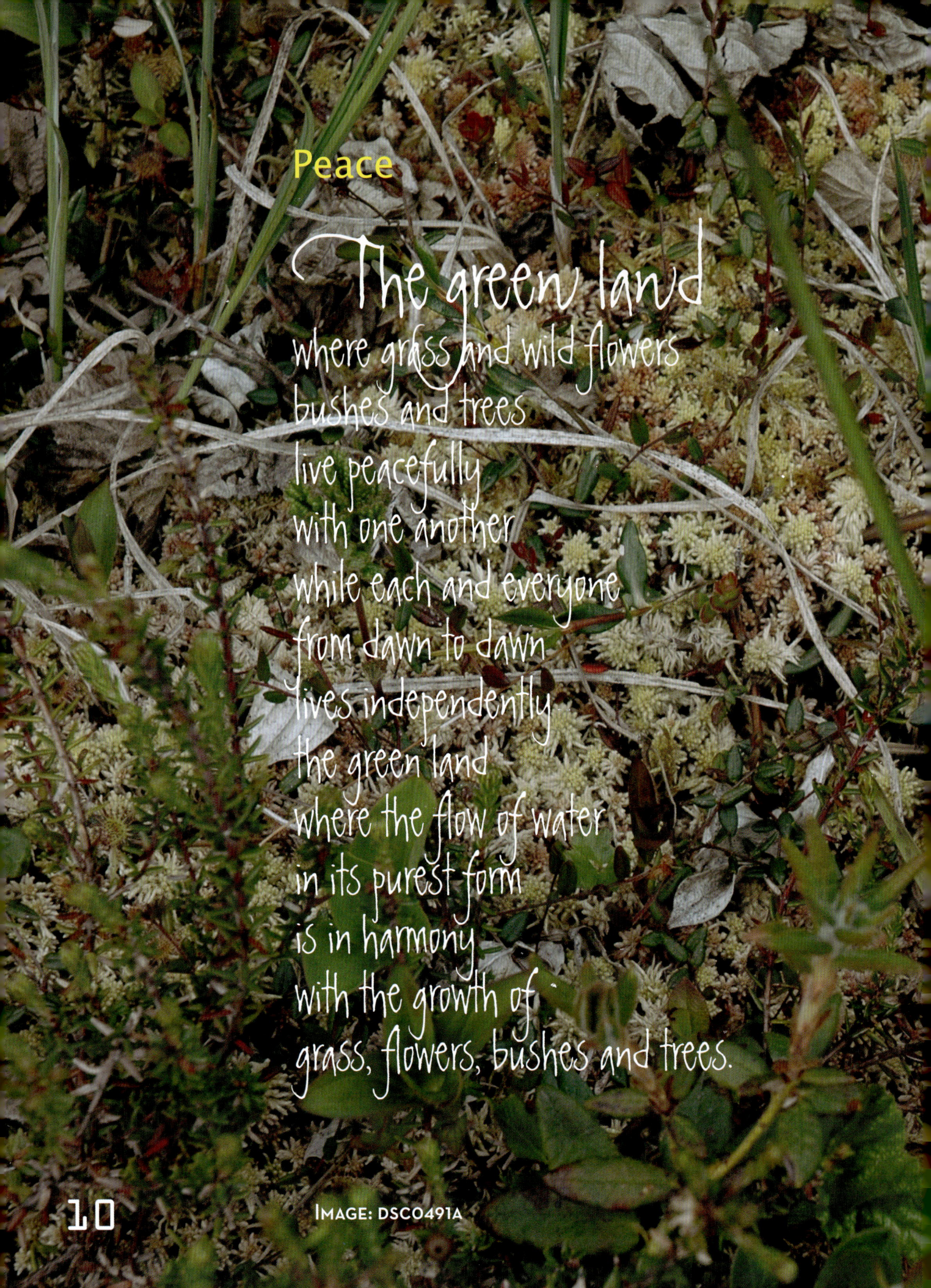

Peace

The green land

where grass and wild flowers
bushes and trees
live peacefully
with one another
while each and everyone
from dawn to dawn
lives independently
the green land
where the flow of water
in its purest form
is in harmony
with the growth of
grass, flowers, bushes and trees.

The solid rock

The solid rock
beneath my feet
had nested a seed
in its open heart
keeping it away
from the cruelty
of coming, freezing day

Then in one sunny day
a flower grew
out of the rock's heart
gently it spoke
of its unique life
within a stone made heart
it said, I have lived
in the heart of a rock
but secure, indeed

As I walked away
from the solid rock
I stepped into a desert land
that was covered with sand

Then I realized
how soft hearted are
the solid rocks
that allow a seed
to nest within them
and how far they will
go
to help a seed grow.

The beauty of life

Sometimes I like to burst
into tears
and sometimes
I like to burst out the fears
that I feel
when I tell the truth
about the roots of love
that I feel
for many, many people.
Sometimes I like to see
people grow
as the flowers do.
And this time
I am not to see
but I am to be
a part of you.
I am to be

a flower in the garden
growing there with you.
The beauty of life
is in sharing and caring
and I am here to share
and I know I care
for all of you
dear people.

Cruel Cycle

There was a bird
by the sea
sitting, hoping
there will be fish
for him to prey
not knowing
there is a fish
in the water
watching him
and wondering why
One has to die
for one to survive.

You are now in my heart

With my eyes closed
I go to sleep
and dream of you.
I see you dancing
in an angel's dress
walking on the ocean
just like the sun rays.
And when I am awake
your picture is in my eyes
and I see you clearly.

Now that you are going away
to seek other eyes,
please remember
the tears through my eyes
carry you with them
into the ocean
through a path in my heart
with no regret or doubt
I would like to shout
you are now in my heart
forever as a friend.

Image: silotest005

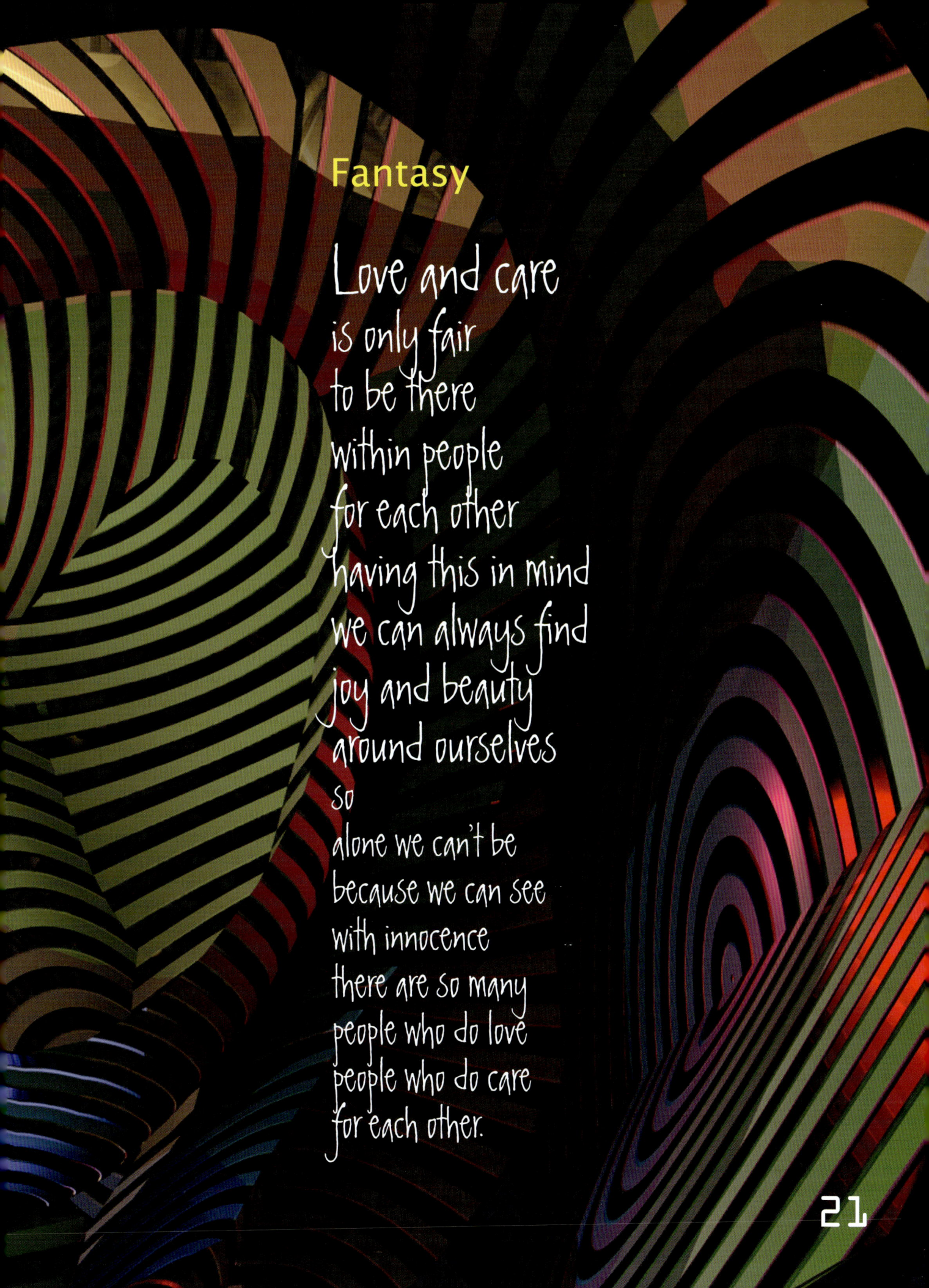

Fantasy

Love and care
is only fair
to be there
within people
for each other
having this in mind
we can always find
joy and beauty
around ourselves
so
alone we can't be
because we can see
with innocence
there are so many
people who do love
people who do care
for each other.

Hope

When the
moon cries
and the tears are felt
by innocent eyes
When the stars
Start falling one by
one
When silence is loud
and the depth of sky
seems as mirage

I feel lost within
the universe of being
Yet I know the sun will shine
and show me the path
through which I'll find
the secrets of life.

Internal treasures

Shadows of fear
slowly appear
in human minds
Fear of death
Fears that symbolize
the need for security
Fear of getting old
Fear of being poor
Fear of reaching out
are slowly causing
humans to decay.

Image: bridge.esch.010a

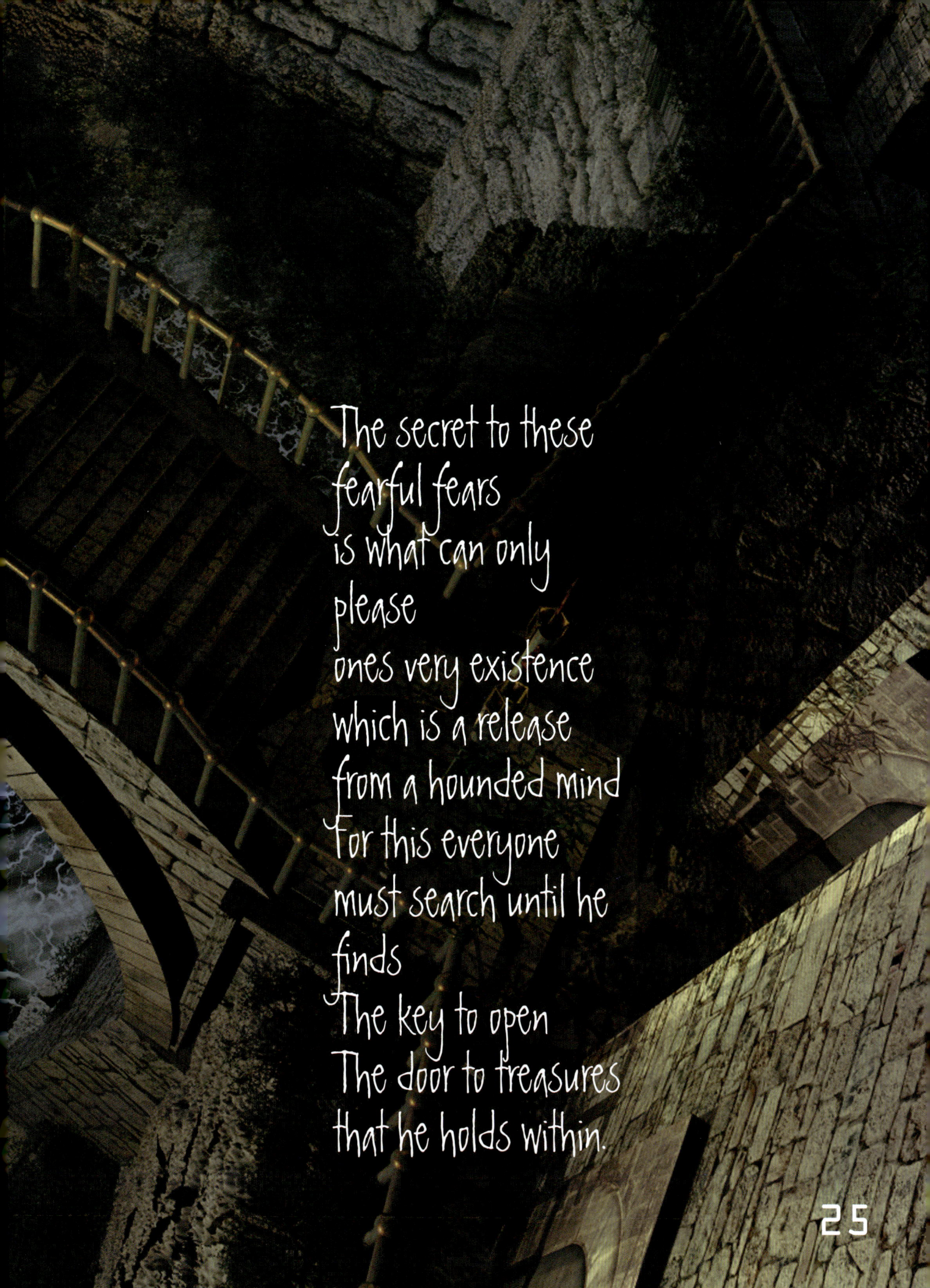

The secret to these
fearful fears
is what can only
please
ones very existence
which is a release
from a hounded mind
For this everyone
must search until he
finds
The key to open
The door to treasures
that he holds within.

Limits of Life

There is no mountain
that we cannot climb
There is no ocean
that we cannot swim
There is no sky
that we cannot fly through
There is no limit
for me or for you.

Image: organotowers.005a

Exposure

The globe is the probe
that examines me
wishing to know and see
the variety
in life styles
in the land marks
and in thoughts

there is no routine
visible to my eyes
even if I see
the same thing twice
each has its own value
short sighted
short minded
brave or different
I am the man
who has been probed
by the globe of thoughts

Image: planetoid.001a

Only you

At the times
when I feel lonely
I seek you
and you only

At the times
at the darkest night
when I seek for light
at any point of my
mind
I look for you
until I find
you, and you only

Image: D1335C

We all are one

Regardless of
who you are
I love you
Regardless of how
you think
I love you
Regardless of any-
thing
I love you
Because you are me
and I am you
and this is why

I love you.

Friendship through my eyes

Be there

where I need you to be
and I will be
where you need me to be.

Free from all boundaries
Memories of laughter
and happy times
can be shared

Then at the sad times
I will be there
You will be there
Where we need to be.

Experience

Loving one is done
Through eyes and
heart and soul
with purified love
we can create
a world of happiness
a world of pleasure
that we can treasure
throughout our lives
forever and ever.

Loving one is done
through understand-
ing
through feeling
through sharing
all that mind can see
with all that one can be
and all there is in life
in a perfect life
one should live to love
as mentioned above.

The structure of love

Love was never
born
and it will never die
it is never young
and it doesn't grow
old
it will never give
and it doesn't take
it isn't ocean
nor is it a lake
it's always true
so it can't be fake
it can't be predicted
nor one gets ad-
dicted

Image: DSC0674E

to the love I mean
to the love I know
Love is never bought
nor could it be sold
it never gets hot
it never gets cold
Love could not be
fate
it's never early
and it doesn't come
late
it is always there
within the people
who love everyone.

It matters not

It matters not
I am short or tall
or I am white or black
it matters not
I am a man or woman
nor it matters
if I am a beach
or a grain of sand
what matters
is we stand united and tall
as human beings in history
have risen to find out
they will fall.
It matters not
what we have done
or what our elders did
what matters is
can we stand
giving without expectation to
receive

It matters not
who said what
what matters is
what was said
It matters not
who is alive in flesh
but dead in soul
what matters is
that the flesh and
soul are alive
It matters not
if you were the only
one
who survived a ho-
locaust
or lived alone in a
crowd
what matters is
that we voice our
love
for mankind aloud.

The moral of this poem
is not what matters
or what matters not
But it is to bring
a new message
to all human beings
the moral of this poem is
live and aim to please
all human beings
black, white, young or old
we may be different
in our bodies or colors
but we all have the same
soul
It matters not
who is who
or who did what
what matters is
we all care about
one another
share with each other
in an equal way
in our journey to the des-
tiny.

My Mind

It is too small to grow big
and it is too big to grow small
It is an epigraph
somewhere in a town
waiting to be engraved upon
It is a spring
flowing down from the mountaintop
hoping to quench the thirsty.

The road towards unity

Let your ears hear
and not fear the confrontation with truth.

Let your eyes see
the depth of innocence
and the true value of love.

Set your body free
to touch, to feel
the unity of humanity.

Image: mosquewell.019

Fear

This strange feeling
that forces man to obey
and takes away
the purity of life,
that takes away
the capacity to see
the ultimate beauty
of living free
This strange word
is the creator of slavery

The flight towards oneness

Through an open window
the wind blows
into my room
And carries with it
a silent message
From the flowers
that grow
and I don't see
From the birds
that fly
in the vast sky
and I don't hear
And from the distant people
that I don't feel.

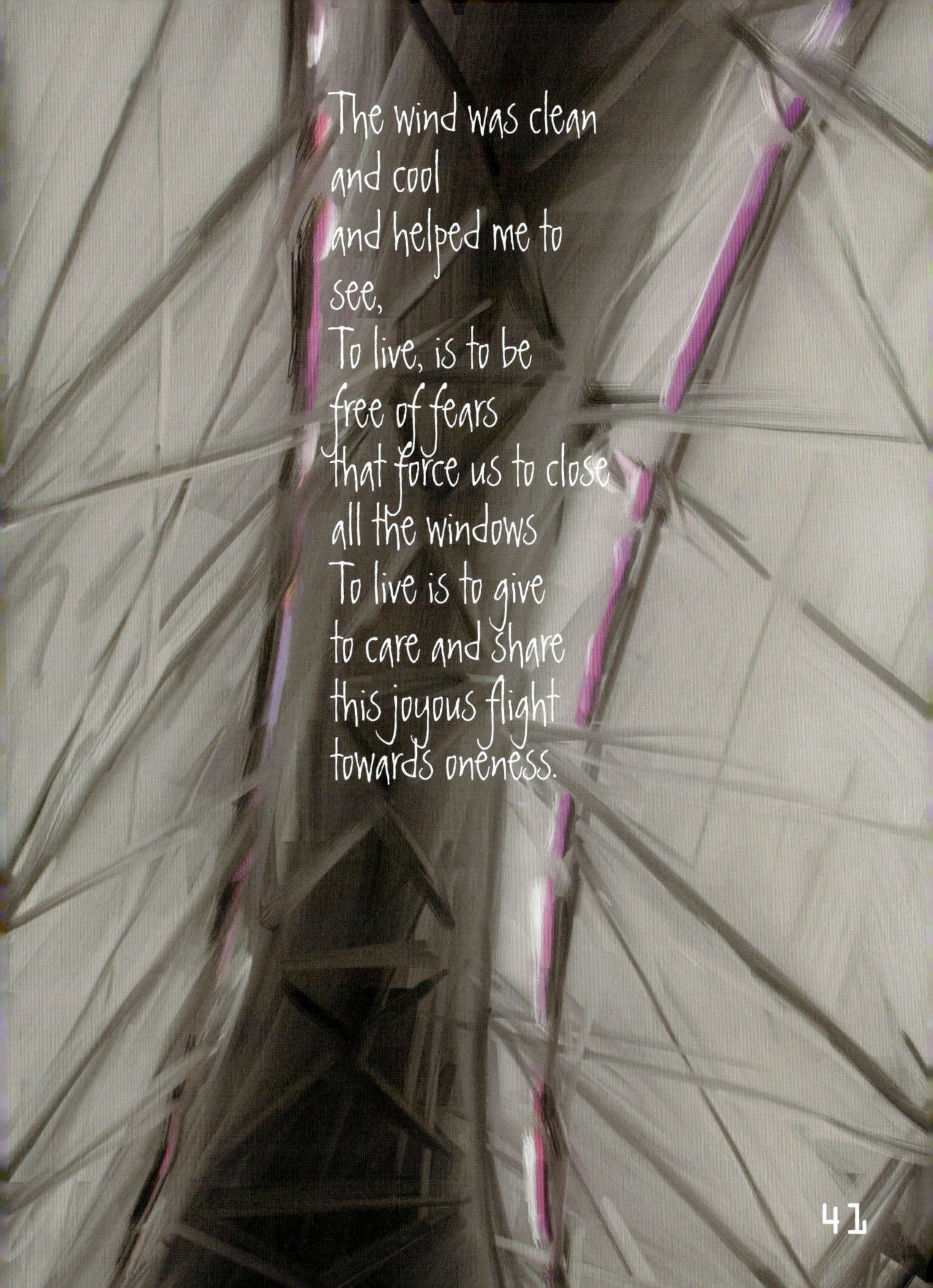

The wind was clean
and cool
and helped me to
see,
To live, is to be
free of fears
that force us to close
all the windows
To live is to give
to care and share
this joyous flight
towards oneness.

Ambitious but lonely

The road is dark and slippery
Sun is hidden behind the earth
and the moon sliding gently behind the clouds.
A lonely man trembling on the pavement of streets,
listening to the beats of his heart,
until they stopped,
and he died...

I am happy

I am happy
to be alive
I am happy
to be, a human
I am happy to know
you exist
I am happy to know
love exists
I am happy to know
there is a sun
that shines day and night
with doubt
I asked myself
I am happy to know
I am a father
even though
I am happy to know
I was once a child
I am happy
to be me
I am happy
because my pen
is able to write

I am happy

do I really know
what is happiness
and my answer is
I am happy to know
I am happy

I am happy to know
there is air
so I can inhale
the love
that you all wish
to spread through the air
I am pleased
I am happy
because I have felt I will
not be defeated
by lack of light
I am happy
when it's dark
I am happy
when there is sun
I am happy
when it rains

I am happy
when it snows
I love the hail
and sun
brings me more happiness
I am happy
I have a pen
so I can write
with my hands
left and right

I am happy
I will age as I grow
I am happy
there are trees
bushes, flowers and
peas
I am happy
because I know
I am alive
and I will grow
like the grass
and like a tree
I am happy
just to be
I am happy

Love comes through within

For a while I thought
the world is too small
the first time I ever flew
leaving "home"
to seek and search
for loving friends

And I found
love comes through
within,
like the water
through a spring;
others can drink
or can swim
in the water
pouring from the
spring
so pure and clean
that the bottom can
be seen.

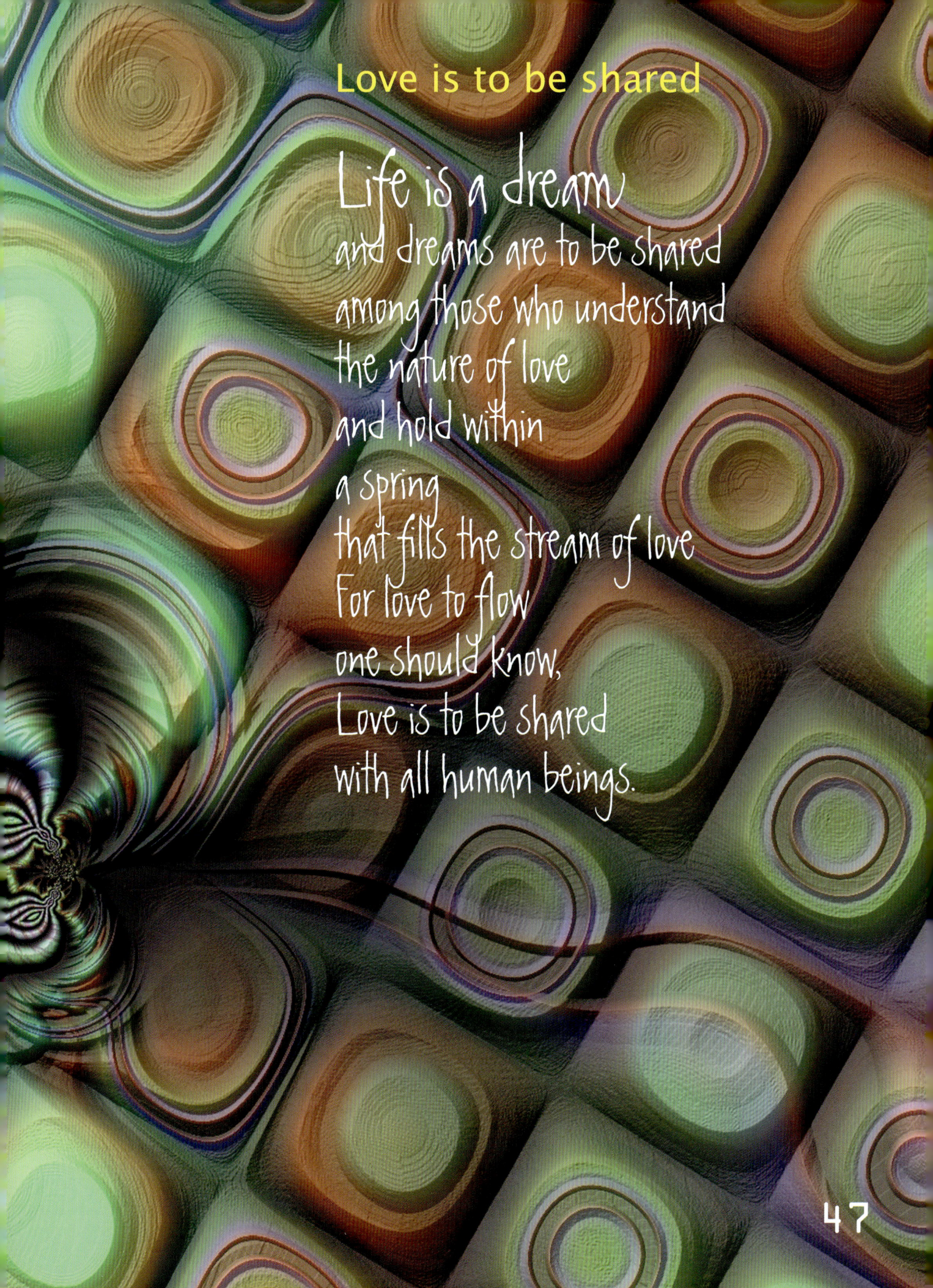

Love is to be shared

Life is a dream
and dreams are to be shared
among those who understand
the nature of love
and hold within

a spring
that fills the stream of love
For love to flow
one should know,
Love is to be shared
with all human beings.

Fruitless tree

A tree
that bears no fruit
is not a fruitless tree
in the eyes of a visionary
who can see
the fruits of a so called
fruitless tree.
I have seen many
who hate an apple
but live under the shadow
of an apple tree.
There are times
that one can see
with closed eyes,
and there are times
that the widest eyes
can not see,

A tree that bears no fruit
is not a fruitless tree.

Drifters Drift

Drifters drift
in the orbit
as if you knew
the things you don't know
and you have heard
the sound of sunshine
but you can't believe
because it isn't even dawn

Image: amsterdam005

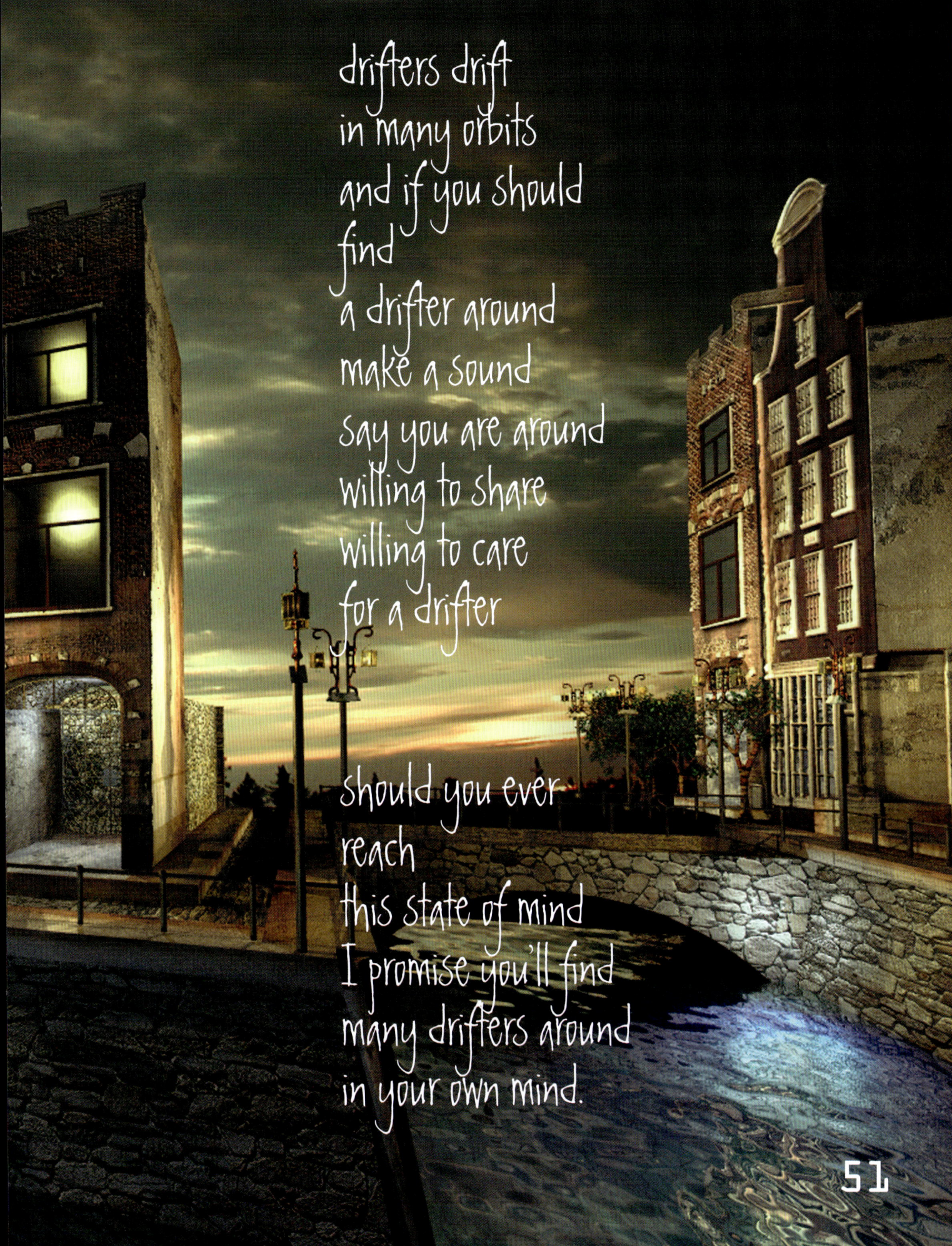

drifters drift
in many orbits
and if you should
find
a drifter around
make a sound
say you are around
willing to share
willing to care
for a drifter

should you ever
reach
this state of mind
I promise you'll find
many drifters around
in your own mind.

Be Fair

I write this poem
in a moment of pain
I thank you
for the champagne
but not the rain of thoughts
happy, mad, angry or sad
that you fed to my mind
I wish now to close
this chapter
leave behind
your gift to my mind

so go away
live alone
you may someday find
the you that you left behind
but if I should
care to share
I wish to request
that you be fair
to the next drifter.

The Turbulent Mind

Fasten the seat belt

said the sound
turbulent thoughts
are coming our way
from strange minds
I felt at ease
since I have often been pleased
with turbulent thoughts
or sparks within my own mind
so I did not feel bounded and exposed my mind
to the turbulent thoughts

one interesting thought
was about
this fish that could talk
he told me stories
about all the creatures
who live under water
he told me about
the river fish
who moved to the ocean
against his parents will
then he told me about
how nice life is
in the water
there are no politics
there are no lies

no one deceives
no one steals
no one is homeless
everyone obeys
the one and only rule
for all who live
in the water
he said
we all live and believe
in ourselves
then he apologized
because he had to go

then there was
this other thought
that shook my mind
the thought of being
the only human being
who lives on the earth

what would I do
with all the wealth
with all the room
but no one to share
think about it
what would life be like
if you had no one to talk to
no one to love, but yourself

The sound said again
we are through
the turbulent thoughts
we will shortly land
so prepare yourself
with your heads upright
and your thoughts straight

The Secret of Life

At the time
When It's not day or night,
At the time
When it's not soon or late,
At the time
When the heart leads the mind
And the mind leads the heart,
At the time
That moments are centuries,
I feel released
Because it's at that time
That I see me
Who is free,
Who can love,
With no restrictions,
Who can fly in the sky
Just like a dove

Image: boolyeggs003a

Above the boundaries
That man has set before himself
To fall on his own knees
And has built a prison
Which contains
Contagious disease.
It's at that time
That I can see
The harmony
between love and me
And I can hear
The secrets of life

I Kissed You

I kissed you
and my lips turned red
I missed you
and my heart felt dead
and my mind
interpreted both and said
treasure what you feel
for your feelings are real.

The wise thorn

I am not a thorn
attached to the stem
that holds and protects a rose
nor am I a thorn
in the eyes of visionaries
I am a thorn
to be held and felt gently
for I only wish to be
an awakening thorn
to help everyone to see
the rainbow of life
and the depth of universe
that each and everyone
dearly holds within

Tears

Two globes of light
that are shiny like diamond
that are like
two mountains of snow
that resemble thousands of
unspoken stories
or like two trees
that hold enormous number of
green, yellow or brown leaves
or perhaps two drops of ink
for writing stories
that have rooted in our hearts
that explain the past
that show the love
or represent happiness

These two drops of water
are always there
and ready to speak
of hidden secrets
that we hold within.

The Windows

The windows

have opened to me
and I can hear
the gentle whisper
of my lover;
the nature
sitting here on a rock
surrounded by trees
I feel ecstasy
the river before me
is the river of life
the mountain beneath my feet
is the peak of life
from here I can see
the depth of universe within me

Image: hoohouse001a

The Cat

The cat
who touched the moon
owed the achievement to the dog
who chased her out
the comfortable room
that she lived in.
and when the cat returned
she taught the mouse
how to grow wise
her advice to the mouse was
we need to reach out
with a fearless mind
for it's only then
when we can find and touch
the stars, and the moons
that we often dream of

A hollow in space

Shadows of clouds, spreading
darker and darker
with no light around
seems my mind has found
the clouds to leave behind.
A hollow in space
carries a trace
of sadness on its face
and the Earth
wandering around,
like a lost ship in space
beneath my feet
its trembling
and I feel alone
No further, am I able
to direct this wandering ship.
I am lost
in the space
which carries a trace

Image: Solidabstract.002a

of sadness on its face.
The path seems dark and deep
and I am to seek
a way to save this ship
that carries me with it.

The Joy of Flight

The Earth below
and the stars above
riding on the wings of a
dream
I beam my eyes
to the near and distant
land
searching my sole and
body
for the significance of me
living, laughing, thinking
and trying
to move the clouds
from the hidden heavens
that I hold in my soul
touching, feeling and
foundling
with the love
that I feel for human be-
ings
with the earth below

and stars above
like a white dove
I often travel
through the hidden lands
and hold hands
with truth, destiny and life
sharing with all
the joy of my flight
from earth to stars

Image: bigtruss001

The Origin

It is fun to know
the burning candle
provides light
as does the shining sun

It is fun to know water turns to clouds
perhaps the same way as doubts
grow in human mind
clouds travel through skies
then return to earth
in the different forms
rain, hail or snow
they eventually go
to the origin
just like the thoughts
of human beings

or the feelings
we each hold within
it is fun to know
and learn how to grow
become like a candle
or the shining sun
or like the clouds
yet never forget
the origin

A larger life

How can I depict
the spring
that you bring
into my life
the gesture on your face
shows a trace of love and happiness
how can I describe
the tingling love
that I feel
when I see you laugh
so innocently
how can I paint
your beautiful face

that radiates
a larger life
than I can ever live
well
in a simple way
let me say
the smile that you share
with me everyday
gives meaning to life
that I live day by day

Reflection

I often find me
In you
whomever you may be
feeling like the light
weightless and fast
I travel through
present and past

Image: bflowers006

with all of you
So who could "me" be
the you on the earth
the you on the moon
or the you that I hold
within
I have seen you
I have felt you
I have lived with you
awake and in my dreams
I have seen you
in the mirror of life
and I am convinced
that you are me
and I am you
we are actually one
interpreted as two
just remember
that I love you

The Universe Within Me

Deep down inside
I feel like an ocean
which holds glories

Way far outside
I feel like clouds
moving all the time
until they turn to rain

And with life
I feel like the universe
which holds
everything there is

Image: cloakedRoom.012x

Birth of a Thought

This is not to impose
nor is it to propose
acceptance of a thought
that has sparked
in my mind,
but it is to merely expose
the birth of a thought
this is not intended
to change the rules and laws,
but it is to give reason
to the existence of flaws
and if it should be accepted,
then the birth of new laws
is not plausible, but possible.

Image: AMJJ3.020.A

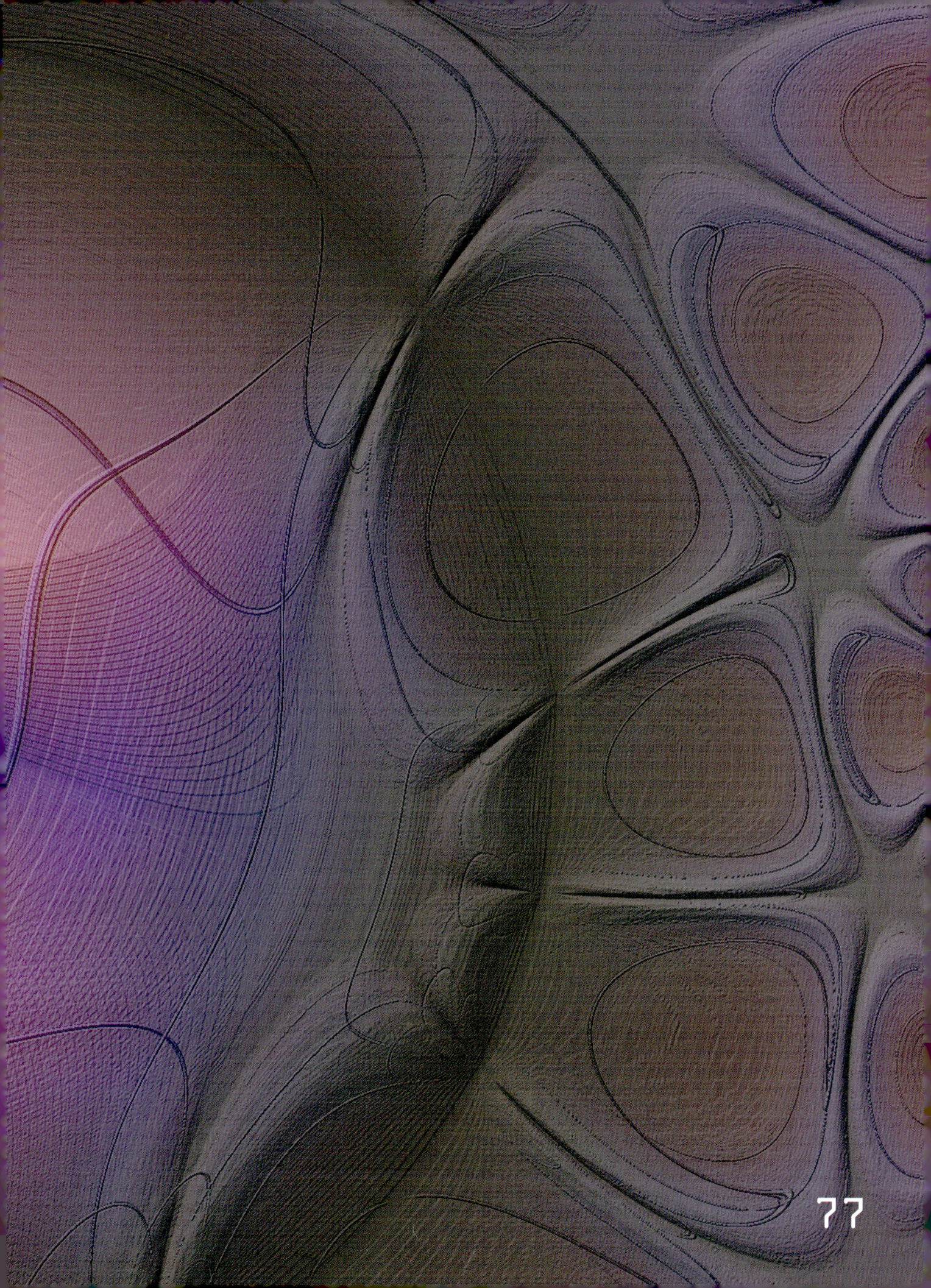

The Old Man

The old man
with a shaking hand
and blue deepened eyes
looked at me and said
life is like the Earth
rotates around itself
as well as the sun

Image: hibayMecha.007

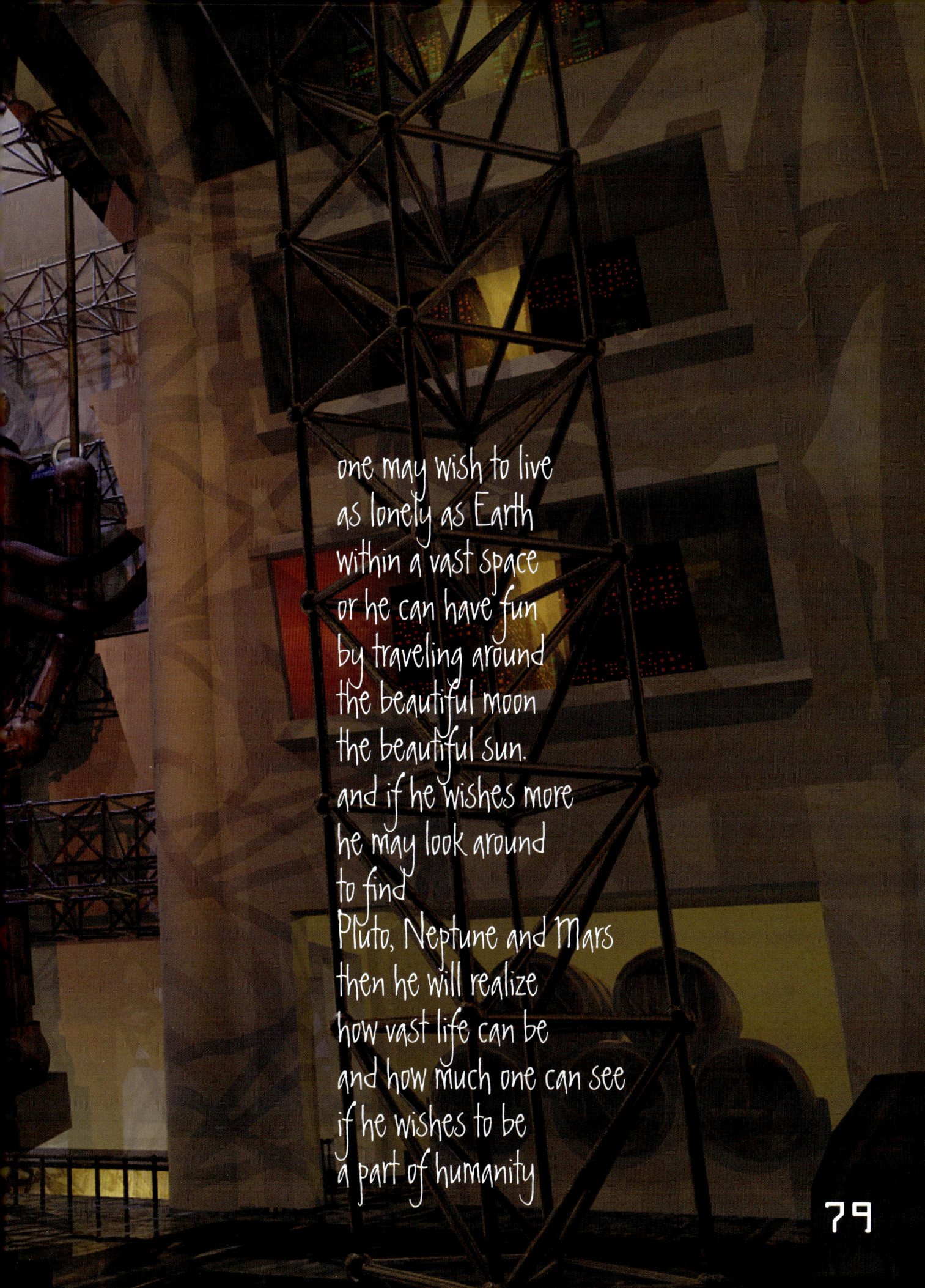

one may wish to live
as lonely as Earth
within a vast space
or he can have fun
by traveling around
the beautiful moon
the beautiful sun.
and if he wishes more
he may look around
to find
Pluto, Neptune and Mars
then he will realize
how vast life can be
and how much one can see
if he wishes to be
a part of humanity

A Shattered Mind

A shattered mind
in harmony with a broken heart
equipped with gun
is blamed for killing many
in a high school
Crying mothers and fathers
saddened neighbors
a nation in mourn
jails are all filled
and more are being built
drugs, guns and fraud
In every town, city and state
in the country
growing faster than trees
the bone structure of our society

Image: gantrypit.003

the family
disappearing slowly
Kidnappers steal our children
killers kill our children
drug dealers addict our children
pimps betray our children
our elders are housed
away from family
In the nursing homes
cheated, mistreated and hardly visited
our elders too die in pain
who is left but you and I
slaved by corporate America
working, 5, 6, or 7 days a week
Hooked with pagers, cell phone
travelling east, west, south and north
we rarely get to know
how our children grow
with fear we live
we need to wake up
and rebuild our lives
weld our families
back together

Cemeteries

Cemeteries
where the dead are alive
and the alive are waiting to die.
People come and go
and they all wonder why
their dear one had to die.
They too fade away
not knowing
that cemeteries
are not a place to pleased.
It's where the "dead ones"
buried under dirt
and covered with a carved rock
are released
and the dead walking ones
are getting ready.
Is the scenery
when to be free
is the time of delivery
or transition.
In cemeteries
trees stand high
green or dry
they supply
a place for birds
to build their nest
fly around
and sing their manifest

Cemeteries
where the doors are locked
and the locks are rocks
but the rocks are fake
just like a lost lake
beyond the mountains
beyond the clouds
or like an ocean
with no water.
In cemeteries
moon doesn't exist
and sun
is just a dying candle
but it can handle
to provide light
for those
who have open eyes
and they can see
the difference
between a living dead one
and an alive in bed
covered with pounds of dirt.
In cemeteries it rains
and washes the pain
off earth's face.

The heart of my soul

The color of my soul
is a rainbow color
touching the horizons of life
the sound of my soul
can be heard from millions of miles away
and I say
welcome to my heart

and the smell of my soul
is heavenly
spreading the scent of love
that I wish to share
with those who dare and care
about human race
would you like to smell, hear or see
my humble soul
or would you like the thought?
the thought of having passed
by the dust
that wind of life
blew in your way
an invitation
to the heart of my soul

The Rainbow

The rainbow
Colorful, happy and silent
Spreads love and hope
On the face of earth
Often at the saddest times
It shines
All over the world
from horizon to horizon
spreading the blanket of
love
then
silently it disappears

giving reason for hope
of coming back again
helping those who need
the rainbow of their life

the rainbow of my life
is the love I feel
for the human race
often aiding me
to find the soul
of humanity in me
the rainbow of my life
is the sun, the moon
the earth and the stars
and everything within
which I want to share
with all those who care

In the garden of life

A rose grew
before my eyes
as I was walking
in the garden of life
Since then I have realized
the beauty of life
is in searching within
and finding the roses
like the ones I have seen
nourish and cherish
each and everyone
of the roses you find
until you develop
a rose garden within your heart.

Friendly Advice

A rose grew
before my eyes
then I felt wise
and gave my friends
rose life like advice
Let your life to be
as the life of a rose
beautiful while alive.

Where all the Angels Fly

I sit here at night
and turn on the light
of loving mankind within me
with my eyes closed
I see the angels dancing
I see the waterfalls
where the angels swim
I see the flowers
that the angels wear as their cloths
I hear the birds sing
the music to which
the angels dance
In a very gentle way
they asked me to say
if I wish to join
their beautiful day
with an open heart
and a decorated mind
I felt I have found
the land where dreams come true

In this beautiful scene
I look for you
my dear angel of life
I dream of you
I want to hold you tight
give you a gentle kiss
and bring in peace
as a gift to you
surrounded with light
with no shadow of doubt
say that I love you
dear angel of life

Then I open my eyes
foolish or wise
I feel proud
to feel the same
for all the angels
that surround me
after all I know
the love I feel will grow
to be a mountain
where all the angels walk
to be the ocean
where all the angels swim
to be the sky
where all the angels fly
in peace and harmony.

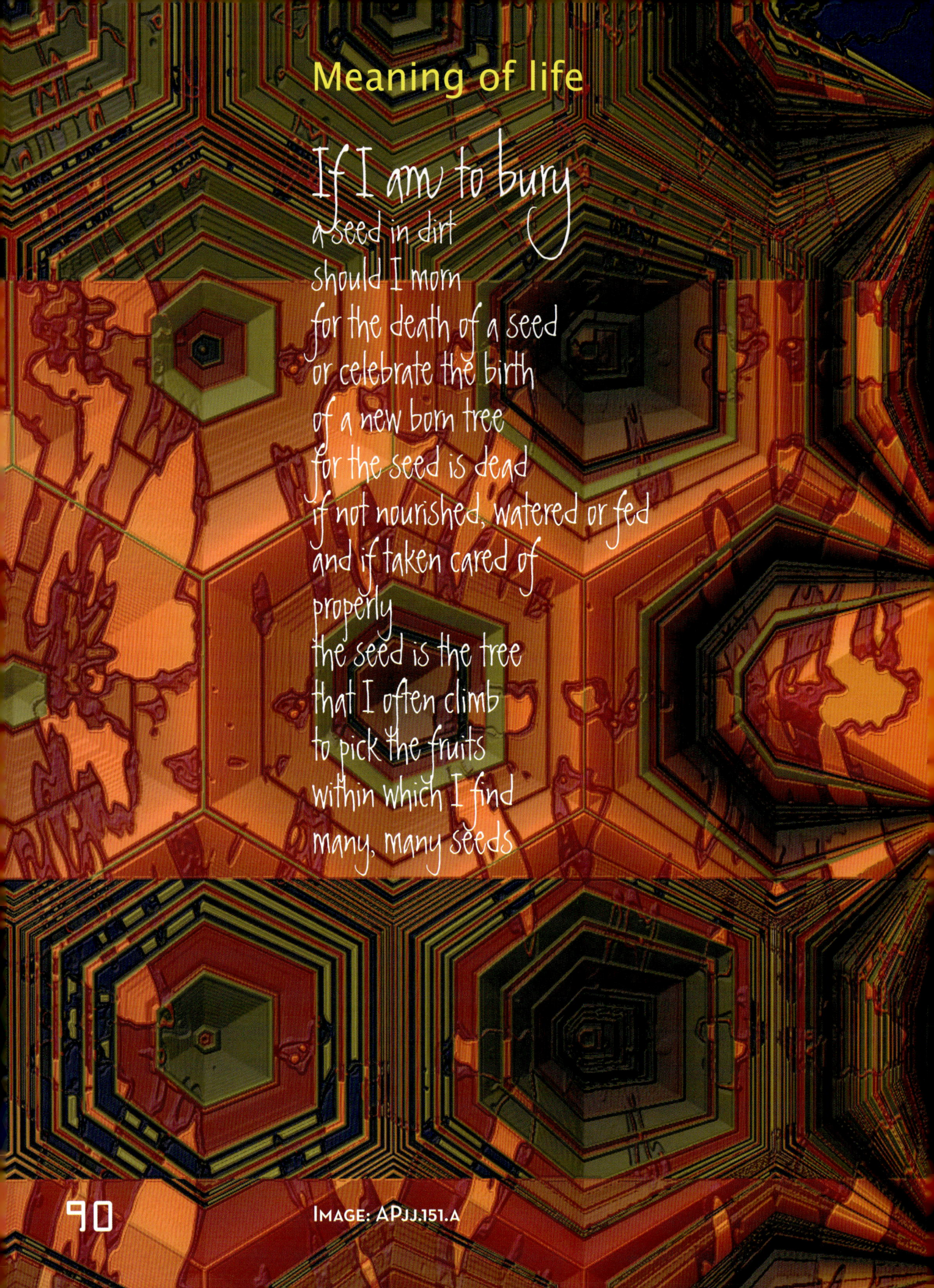

Meaning of life

If I am to bury
a seed in dirt
should I mourn
for the death of a seed
or celebrate the birth
of a new born tree
for the seed is dead
if not nourished, watered or fed
and if taken cared of
properly
the seed is the tree
that I often climb
to pick the fruits
within which I find
many, many seeds

Treasures Within

Treasures Within
are like a spring
buried deep in the earth
unknown to mankind
yet given a chance
they flow
and quench the thirsty

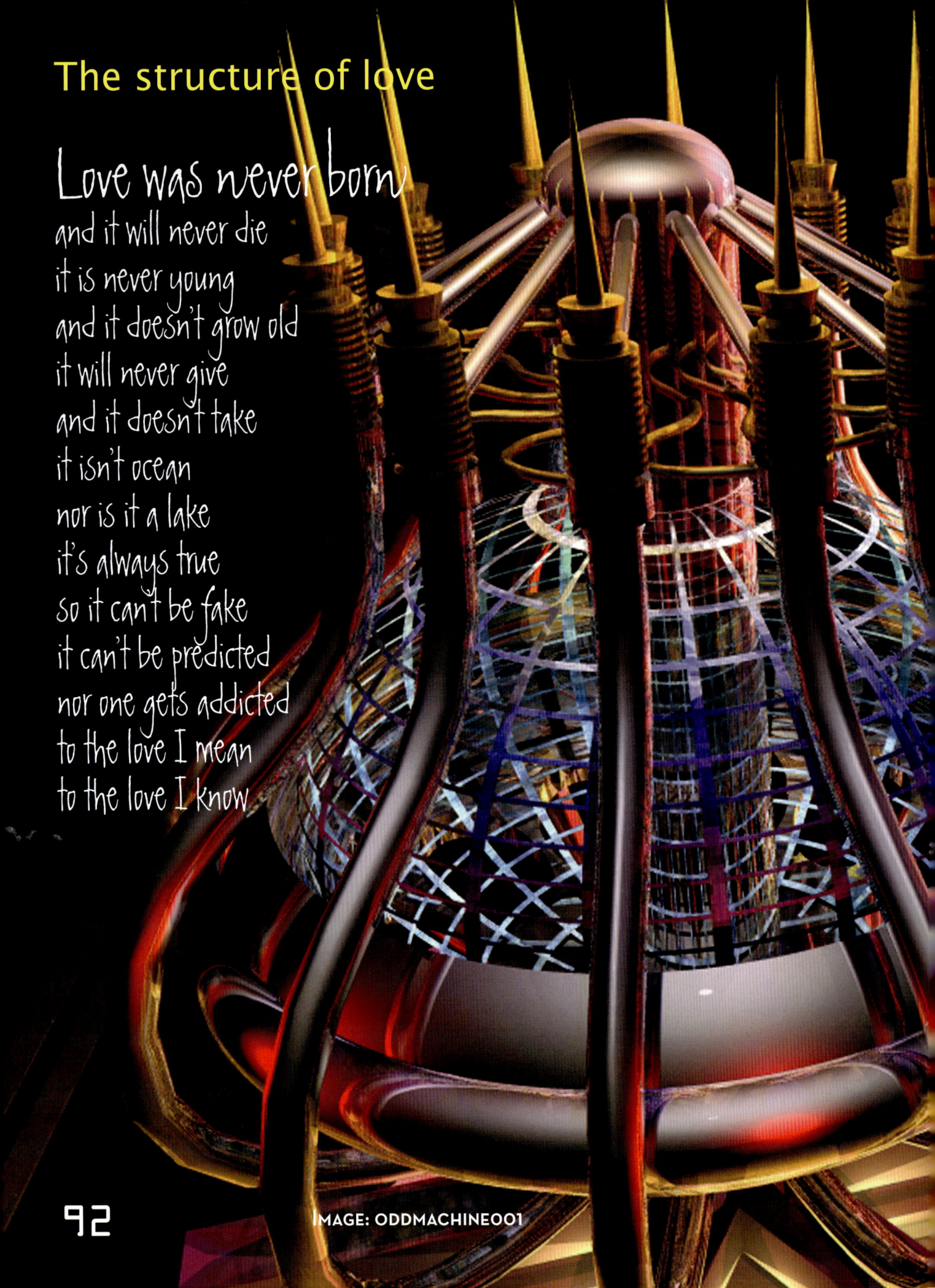

The structure of love

Love was never born
and it will never die
it is never young
and it doesn't grow old
it will never give
and it doesn't take
it isn't ocean
nor is it a lake
it's always true
so it can't be fake
it can't be predicted
nor one gets addicted
to the love I mean
to the love I know

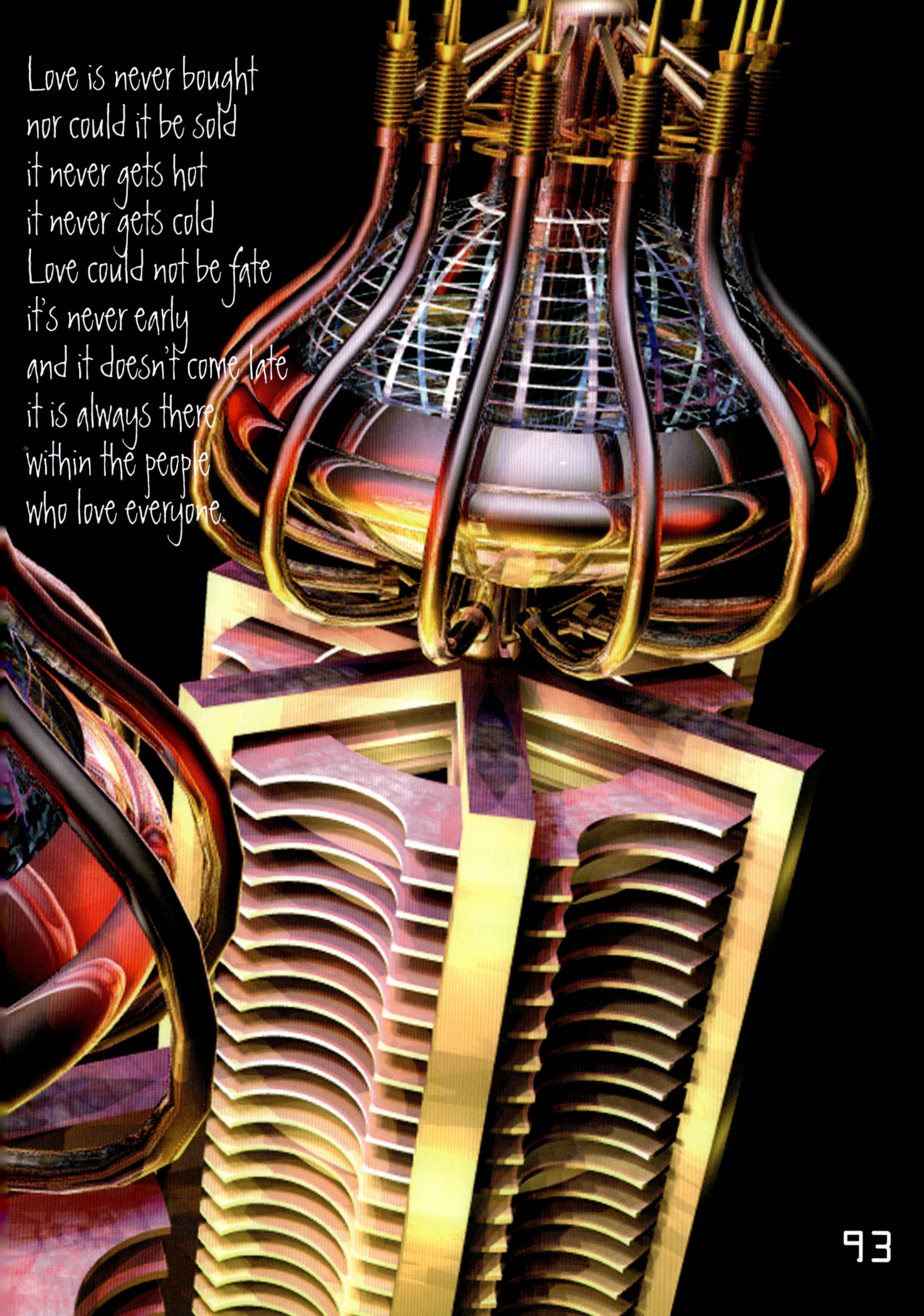

Love is never bought
nor could it be sold
it never gets hot
it never gets cold
Love could not be fate
it's never early
and it doesn't come late
it is always there
within the people
who love everyone.

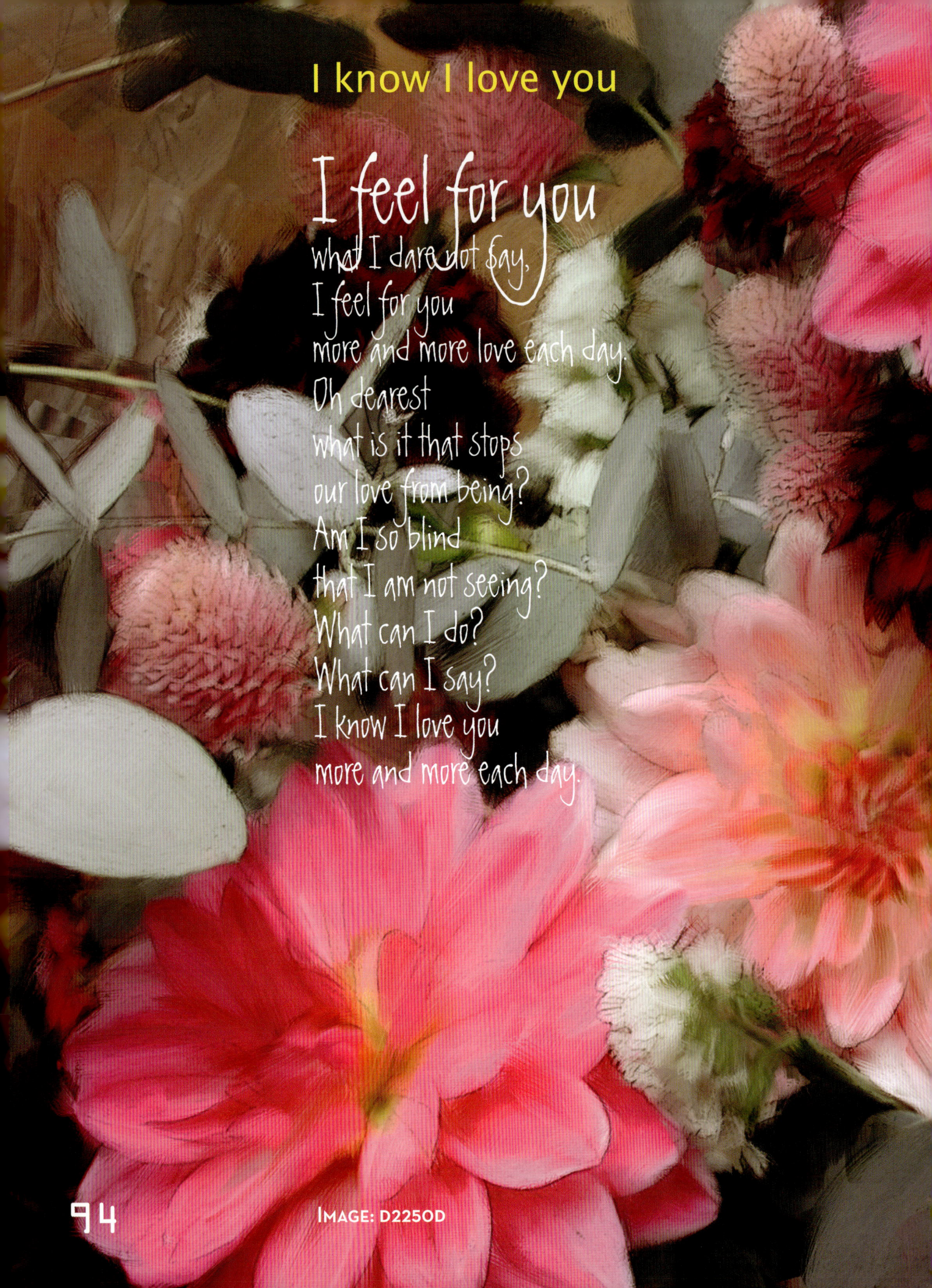

I know I love you

I feel for you

what I dare not say,
I feel for you
more and more love each day.
Oh dearest
what is it that stops
our love from being?
Am I so blind
that I am not seeing?
What can I do?
What can I say?
I know I love you
more and more each day.

Father I am proud

You left us behind
with a thought in mind
for as long as we shall live
we should believe
in loving everyone
in a peaceful world
and we will carry
the flag of love
that you have plant
within our hearts

IMAGE: splineObject007

You thought us to be
free of earthy things
and grow the wealth within
for all human beings
this love that you rooted
in our hearts, is there
for you and all those
who are within this world.

in your memory
my dear father
I promise to carry
the flag that your father
passed on to you
and the flag that you left
for us to carry
the flag of peace,
unity and justice
Oh dear father

Hello Ocean

Once again
I have come to you
wishing to be held
by your open heart
once again
with a heart full of pain
I have come to you
to shed my tears
and share with you
the reasons
in silence.

I Have Given Myself to the Ocean

I have given
myself
To the ocean to take me
Through the paths
Not yet discovered
In this journey
The ocean taught me
How to see
The color of my soul
Such a delight
To see the moonlight
Within the darkness of night

I have given myself
To the ocean to take me
Through the paths
Not yet discovered
During the stormy nights
When the swells were huge
And the winds, exceedingly fast
Ocean held me tight
While teaching me
With a happy voice
In life you have choice
You can sit and see
Your life go by
Or get up and live
Your dream life

Ocean helped me see and feel
The significance of peace
The significance of love
The significance of unity and justice
Within me

I have given myself
To the ocean to take me
To the distant land
Where differences are insignificant
And I am able to meet
People from different lands
The ocean helped me feel and see
The elegant universe
We all hold within
Ocean helped me understand
The unified laws
Of spirit, soul and mind

I have given myself
To the ocean
For the time being

The Parallel Universe

In a grain of sand
I saw the life
I felt the hope
that man holds within

In a flake of snow
I saw the moon
I saw the stars
some very near
and some far away

In a drop of rain
I found life
the universe within
and the universe outside

Image: improbable xxLsat

Colophon Fonts
Title Lucida Grande
Poems Sketchley (BitStream)
Info NeutraFace (House Industries)

Zia Oboodiyat

ZINSTEINE@AOL.COM

Zia Oboodiyat was born and raised in Iran, at the age of 20 he came to United States to further his education. Zia graduated from the school of engineering at San Diego State University. He continued his studies in management and organizational development & received his Masters Degree in 1978. Having traveled all over the world, he quickly realized that people everywhere starve for love and friendship.

For the past many years it has been a dream for Zia to start a foundation for disabled children. Therefore any profits gained from the sale of this book and any contribution received will be applied towards this dream. Send contributions to

Zia Oboodiyat Foundation, 40087 Mission Blvd. Suite 204, Fremont, CA 94539-3680

James J Lemon

LEMONJIM@JJLG.COM

James J Lemon grew up in Indiana, then graduated from Purdue and came to California in 1979. When not working on satellite control center software, Jim likes to make graphic art projects such as this book. Jim made the art and the layout at home on trusty Macintosh computers using custom apps, Bryce, ArtMatic, Painter, PhotoShop & InDesign. *See lots more of Jim's work at www.jjlg.com*